MW00324669

ABUNDANCE

❧ ❧ ❧

*for Sandra
& Dale —

celebrating
abundance
in our lives —

Love,
Robin*

ABUNDANCE

ROBIN CHAPMAN

WINNER OF THE 2007 CIDER PRESS REVIEW BOOK AWARD

Abundance.

Copyright © 2009 by Robin Chapman.
All rights reserved. No part of this book may be reproduced or utilized
in any manner whatsoever without written permission. except in the
case of brief quotations embodied in critical articles and reviews.
Inquiries should be addressed to:
Cider Press,
777 Braddock Lane,
Halifax, PA 17032, USA
CIDERPRESSREVIEW.COM

First edition
09 9 8 7 6 5 4 3 2 1 0

ISBN: 978-1-930781-03-0
Library of Congress Control Number: 2008935566

Cover art: "Herons Waiting" by Anne Miletich. Private
collection; used by permission of the owner.
Author photograph by Will Zarwell.
Cover design by Caron Andregg.

Printed in the United States of America
at Morgan Printing. in Austin, TX

for Will, John, Josh

CONTENTS

FOREWORD

꒱

I
t would be easy to describe Robin Chapman's *Abundance* as a collection of nature poems; too easy, and ultimately disserving, since this intense, emotional collection so frequently transcends its genre. Chapman interweaves the personal with the objectively experiential so carefully that we lose sight of the 'boundary' between the prairies, marshes, woods and rivers and the lives of those people fortunate enough to be immersed in these landscapes. The narrator ceases to be a mere observer of the natural world; instead she comes to occupy her rightful place as another integral element.

The poems in this collection richly mine often overlooked details of the natural world, wisely juxtaposing them with daily life. Like a landscape photographer, Chapman conveys the narrator's story by the views witnessed, until the collection becomes a celebration of the lost art of leaving the house. She understands the importance of each detail we choose—and of the choosing itself—as in as in "What's Left Out," when she critiques her own notes, and realizes that deer, turtles and rain have taken precedence somehow over lunch. Indeed, loss echoes throughout this book, from the "splintered wood" and "cedar shakes blown / from the shelter's roof" in "The Hill in Marquette County" to the duck floating at the center of "What the Eye Supplies," reduced to a "Parabola of light, / The dark double helix, / And the missing point / At which they meet."

Many of the poems are so brief that they merely provide hints of a scene, ephemeral as fire across the prairie, "a little ripple/Of flame, quickly passing" ("Burning the Prairie"). This works particularly well because it engages the reader with just enough mystery, and uses the context of the surrounding poems to provide a more complete picture. The collection coalesces into one large collage of images, carefully selected from an extended trip any of us could have taken, but so few have. And that seems to be the point–so much of life is consumed and occluded by the very process of living; too often we waste it cooped up working day jobs, vacuuming, paying bills, judging book contests. We miss the abundant world around us because we forget to reckon it, to open our eyes and, as Chapman notes in the stunning poem "Dailiness," "*pay attention, pay / attention, pay attention //* To what is slipping away."

—Caron Andregg & Robert Wynne, *Cider Press Review*

Choose abundance, rather than scarcity.

–JOHN CAGE

THE INLAND SEA

BURNING THE PRAIRIE

It is only a little ripple
Of flame, quickly passing.

Poured out of the nozzle
Of hoses, it runs

Like water across a window pane,
In sudden swings and spurts.

There is a quiet crackle as it goes.
Afterwards, all changed—a light ash,

The blackened ground, blackbirds
Hunting, flame rippling their wings.

FIELD TRIP

We go slowly, look up faces
In our field guide, call out
Names and rumors.
This large dill-like umbel
Could be poison parsnip—
Brush the leaves
On a hot day with a sweaty hand
And it itches for weeks,
Spots the skin brown.
We file its name
With stinging nettle, poison oak,
The perfect white cap
Of the Death Angel, hemlock.

SADNESS

Slow rain, and wind shaking more
from the arborvitae leaves,
small local squalls;
every bloodroot blossom
cupping drops, the blue squills dripping
their own heavy showers,
the daffodils nodding and bending
under the soft blows, the black pollen
of the tulips a streaky kohl—

is that what this sadness is, the weight
of what's falling away
caught, carried a little while, till loss
spills over, soaks the ground,
waters our rooted lives?
                              And where
would the rain come from, if not
from the breath of the sea's live surface,
seeding every drop?

MADISON, 3/8

Dear Ones—I started to call
my mother this morning, to tell
her how I have washed the leaves
of my plants, stacked the sheets,
double and single, fitted and flat,
in my linen closet, bought flour
and chocolate to make cookies to send
to John and Josh—and every act,
like hers, done with double pleasure,
for itself and the result—I wanted
to tell her I finally know, after
all my sulking and blame, how much
she had to teach, and only this afternoon
I found and bought a bathrobe
as soft and warm and wrapped as hers,
in my own bright fuchsia tones, and sat
in my new arm chair, glad, at home,
the way she was after a day
of work and baking, washing, folding,
putting away—done with the annual
spring stripping and rewaxing of floors
on her knees, the fall shopping trip
for patterns and cloth in the Ford
that burned a quart of oil a week—
I reached for the phone to tell her
I had begun to understand how joy
is a way of seeing the world,
before I remembered that I
am older than she was then,
and she already seven years dead.

FOR DINNER WE HAD POTATOES

Boiled, baked, fried, mashed,
Peppered, with onions, hashed,
Parsleyed, whipped, buttered, creamed,
Cubed, scalloped, cheesed,
Twice-baked, pancaked,
New in their skin, vinaigretted,
Moat to hold gravy—my mother
Made them in endless variety,

And I learned to peel,
Mastering the rhythm,
Long strokes of skin, not slicing
The thumb knuckle, a knife
For sunscald spots,
Dimples that could be navels
Called *eyes—must be*
Looking in—I dug them out,
No omphalosceptic, knowing
We wanted two each,
More for the pot.

PRAIRIE

Hairy puccoon is the first flower we learn, coming to the field decades after the failed farmer, its buttery blooms of late May. We are young and giddy with ownership, weighted with field guides, learning where the lady's slippers return each year in the hickory woods, the fern forest grows, the morels rise along the dead elm roots.

In the dry west field the British soldiers, red-tipped fungus like scattered matchsticks, strike the first color; orange flames spread to the patches of summer hawkweed, climb rosy down the stems of blazing star into the fall, finish in the yellow fire of goldenrod. We leave the campfire stew cooking to watch the sunsets.

We pitch a tent, bring friends who swim around the neighbor's pond, help us build a shelter, an outhouse, cook crepes over the coals. Bring our first-born, second-born, to the summer shade of the edging oaks, childhoods among grasses above their heads in rain and wind and mud, our small dog red as a fox trotting on ahead, looking back at us.

We layer our memory of prairie with season, as week by week the same field breaks into a dozen new species of bloom—spiderwort, flowering spurge, penstemon, leadwort. We piece together the photographs—small dots of what the wind has sown, hundreds of new names rising in our mouths.

John Muir grew up two miles from here, followed honey bees over this hill, inventing gadgets in his head, kept walking west to Yosemite, talked Roosevelt into national parks. Here we learn to watch the light in the changing grass, decipher tracks of fox, listen for the sandhill cranes at dusk, trace the stars in a sky so dark that millions shine.

We think it's timeless, like the names in books: the dark, the stars, the calls, the field that holds our lives for a while, green and growing in the sun's bright eye; though we learn to read the shifting shadows of the day, the turning constellations of the night.

BY CAMPFIRE LIGHT

i.m. Betty Alkire

The fire flamed up around the pan,
Your hands worked in and out of flame,
Softened tortillas, folded cheese,
Tested heat by the sound of oil,
Fried quesadillas over coals,
Slid the skillet back to stone.
The light flamed up around your smile,
Your face alight, eyes flickering.
Your hair flamed up about your face,
Its curls escaped and whispering.
We poured out wine and watched you work,
Firelit, starlit, on that dark hill;
The dark flared up about the fire,
The Dipper poured the cold stars out;
We followed the Milky Way to its split
Where you waved and took the other way,
Wheeling into night, the stars, the smoke
Of memory gathered around the fire-ring stones.

TURKEYFOOT

Swollen purple joints, blue stems gone stiff
And red, lifting high above the goldenrod
Three or four scaly toes, blue and wine-rust,

From which spill, one after another, pairs
Of small yellow and purple
Wind-chiming flowers, or the dust

Of their pollen, falling like music
Through the rolling layers
Of prairie grass; or the soft fuzz

That comes after, like foam,
And floats away; or what's left,
Thin gold hairs that held the bells

In the waving seed-feet, the moving sky,
The windy, watery, body of light—
Small, late blooms on an inland sea.

CATTAILS

June cattails ring the marsh,
    doubled cylinders held above
        the new leaf tips—
a chartreuse fuse lit and burning
    down the barrel to the matched
        receptive green that, come fall,
will be all that's left of what we see—
    thick brown plush topped
        by a thin charred stalk.
Come spring again,
    a wild unraveling
        amid the bent old leaves
and tender greens—
    torches that seed the world
        as they disappear.

THE MARSH AS WEATHERCOCK

The marsh knows which way
The wind's blowing; summer's skin
Of duckweed driven to the south shore,
A chartreuse band browning
At the edges; and all the reeds
Bending and sighing, bending and sighing
    Toward the widening water.

WHAT THE EYE SUPPLIES

The duck
Could be drowsing
In the late sun
On the lake,
Resting his head
On his breast,
Lazily looking
For something to eat.

Or is it a duck
Doubled,
Swimming
In twinned symmetry,
Gaze twined
In the creature
At its feet?

Who are they, stopped
In their dreaming?
The instant leaves
Only a streaming
Parabola of light,
The dark double helix,
And the missing point
At which they meet.

IF CRICKETS DIDN'T SING

If crickets didn't sing
So loud, telling how warm
It is, you'd hear quieter things—
Flies landing, flick
Of the frog's tongue,
The heron stepping.

BRAIDING

Our fingers fumble to remember
the motion of our mother's hands at work,
French-braiding on early school mornings
as we choose the stalked tresses of garlic
from the piles stacked on Mary's porch,
ten kinds over-wintering, August-pulled—
we shake off the mud clumped to roots, lay
the pungent cloves along the newest fold, bring
the lowest strand up and over, layer another,
making a loom of our fingers, three women
side by side, gathering the harvest
into heavy plaits to dry; knowing now
it pleased our mother's eye.

PRAIRIE RESTORATION

One by one the prairie species come,
Fill every niche of time and light.
Their names spill into poems on the tongue,
Liatris, aster, needlegrass. We watch

The wash of Renoir's colors through
The bluestem grass, the herons sweeping
Home. In evening light the junipers
Could almost be bison, gently grazing.

BLOODROOT

Who among us knows
as deep in our roots
how ephemeral life is?
Who sheds the winter
as quickly, who in our haste
to bloom thrusts up a face
to the sun, only the sun
and the bees
before we have even unfolded
our hands?
Who praises in our green
open-handedness as gladly?

WILD INDIGO

How plain their intentions,
  slender cream spikes
    held high over spring prairie,

each capsule of bud
  swelling larger
    down the straight stalks

into the full, pouting
  sweet-pea mouths—
    Cupid bow upper lip, swollen pouch—

white flames
  that will be the last
    to wink out in prairie dark;

though these bare stems themselves,
  slender, newly thrust
    through the rooted ground

with that waxy
  untouched blush
    of the very young,

confide, in tender purple underglow,
  it is all
    done for love—

something we might not know
  coming later on the woody branches
    and seeded pods of indigo.

THE EVOLUTION OF SLEEP

Burrowed deep in our bed,
Alligators in river mud,
We bask all night in the other's
Skin spooned back to belly,

Thin reptilian gills remembering
How warmth crept in as Dimetrodon
Raised its long back fin
Into the face of the sun,

Mammalian arms curled round
The other's radiating body,
Man and woman minds
Dreaming mud, dreaming mother,

And the blood-warm plunge of love.

PASSAGE

Something is opening,
A door in the long white corridor

Outside, where grass used to grow
There are trees colored by children

I have shrunk shorter
Than the flowers

Something is opening
In the flowers, their yellow throats

In the tall maples
The sky opens

The rain, the rain
Has turned to leaves

WILD SARSAPARILLA

Trios of mostly five-leafed stems
a foot high under the arborvitae cover—
if we walk here next year and the next,
we'll learn they're not beginning trees
but the understory. Wild sarsaparilla,
ginseng family, we could find in a book
if we looked close enough, and this
is the knowledge of things that allows
the long-dead, whose stories we've lost,
to speak to us in our language—
how the roots, brewed to make a bitter tea,
can cure toothache, sore throat, heart pain.
And the warning: take only the main root,
leave the side roots to restore the harvest.

If we stay with the saw-toothed leaves, rain comes,
filters through the canopy, streaks our faces,
runs down the leaf veining, drips
from the dark purple-black berries.
The red squirrel drops green fronds
of arborvitae at our feet. Sunlight
picks out each one of us for an hour.
Wind comes up in the afternoon.

We breathe and breathe—leaf mold,
mist, hemlock, harebell, fern. Bend
with motion in the air—gull cry,
hummingbird, cicada chirr.
Shade takes in dusk. New creatures
walk. Deep and secret in the root,
a sharp truth concentrates, bittersweet,
that could cure our pain.
Oh, how can we not love our lives?

BOUNDARY WATERS 🌿

WIND IN THE BOUNDARY WATERS

West wind whistles through the woods,
      calling for any loose leaf or old limb
            to come fly with it

over the marshes and bays,
      enters our lake as wrinkles of gust,
            ripples of push, waves that shove

till the shore takes the shock
      and gives it back. The bedrock—granite
            of Canadian shield—cools, gives up its heat.

Wind rattles our ears, tears food from our hands,
      drives off black flies, tugs at canoes,
            loosens our tent stakes,

shoulders its weight against pines, poplars
      drizzling army worms, so that the tallest,
            the heaviest, topple—tip-ups

with their black fans of labyrinthine roots
      and shallow earth exposed to sun,
            dark humps that could be bear or moose.

Only four years ago, a west wind blew
      ninety miles an hour all night,
            a screaming scythe

threshing three million trees
      in the shallow-rooted land. We tie square knots
            and hunker down,

the wind against our faces
      indifferent to us—a touch, a muscled arm, a fist
            of iron.

BOUNDARY WATERS

A wash of rain slants the dark southern sky
    where sunlight detours, glows, and breaks.
        Wild rice unripe in barbed green husks
            bends in the wind that churns whitecaps.

We stand on granite under the double arc of rainbow,
    dripping swimmers come up for air. Our arms
        have pulled us—canoes and gear—through miles
            of water whispering now in our bones. The sky

brightens to evening, the wind's rough tongue
    licks us dry and shivering, the whine
        of mosquitoes reminds us that dusk
            and their kind will settle soon, consign

us to the armor of jackets and DEET,
    tucked in the safety of zippered tents
        to sleep. We boil the water, wolf
            down home-dried hopping john, rinse

dishes, swat, slap, run to our mats
    on stony ground, our dreams of tasks undone.
        Did I say, along this boundary of water and skin
            I am as happy as I've ever been?

CROSSING THE BOG

At every bouncing step we expect to sink,
but—miracle of fibrous mat, we flounder on,
thinking *waterbed*, thinking *we walk on water*
till one or two break through.
                                        Emilie wanders
in her element, speaking Latin to leather fern
and tamarack, rose pogonia spike,
testing the depth of sphagnum moss
that cushions us, sponging twenty times its weight
in water acid as soda pop. She shows us
the cups of the pitcher plants, the only place
where bog mosquitoes breed—carnivores,
like the sticky sundews, where flies feed flower.
Here's community neither land nor lake nor swamp,
bog that could hold a man or woman
in its dark tannin for a thousand years.

We hurry on, gain the lake, reload canoes, ride
them through building waves like horses at full gallop.
Up and down we stretch over the bows,
hurl paddle blades into the steep oncoming rise,
knees braced against their heaving, plunging sides.

MOOSE RIVER

The long watergrass lies down in the current
      moving past us, points the way downstream
as Will and I paddle up-river, wild rice on either side,
      water-lilies and spatterdock. Beaver lodges
broaden the margins as we curve and recurve
      through aspen and pine and alder horizon.
The river vanishes at the corner of sight,
      taking the way that water takes
draining bog and granite, when we see, ahead,
      the young moose, all legs and nose, ears
flicking away black flies, skin shuddering, his muzzle
      dripping with water weeds. He lifts
knobby joints to move another foot, buries his head
      in muck, raises another mouthful, and still
we're paddling closer, silent now, motioning
      to the other canoe. We stop some forty feet away
to watch him browse his way toward shore
      and climb the bank, a wooden marionette
lifted on jerky strings to shoulder his way into woods.
      We paddle on, our wish for a glimpse
of a wild creature granted—how close we came
      to wildness only surfacing at Mary's cabin
a week later, when she tells of canoeing the river,
      her companion's ill-behaved dog
rocking the canoe with his lurches—how they, too,
      came upon a young moose, moved closer—
and from nowhere the mother charged,
      thirty miles an hour toward them
downhill into the water—I thought I was dead,
      said Mary. I could see the hair in her nostrils.
In slow motion she felt the dog stick his head
      under her arm and heard woof!

and the moose halted two feet away from the boat
        and turned back. We thought back to our encounter,
 the tall grass, the flies, the calf, the connection missing
        in our eager heads between a calf and his mother.

THE LONGEST DAY

North Lake to Snow Bay, we stop only to explore
   weed-grown campsites, spread our lunch
      on the Canadian shield–red onions, sausage,
         bread—portage North to South Lake,

Eugene to Gunn, unloading, shouldering the packs.
   Find campers already tucked into all the places
      we'd chosen on the map. We slip
         into Lac La Croix, big water

smooth as glass, take our chances on a long run
   west, steer an exhausted family
      of two canoes, lost and mad, to the next
         fire grill and tent pad,

dodge the seaplanes landing fishermen
   at a wilderness resort, paddle on with wind
      and weather at our backs, trade off bow
         and stern, thread the islands—

voyageurs, our third day out.

MAKING CAMP

Shucking clothes—
        cold shock of dark water,
                fire under the skin

Distant thunder—
        Margaret embroiders a dragonfly
                on her canoer's shirt

Waiting out the storm
        under Will's tarp—we fill
                our cups with rainwater

Walking at dusk—
        we pick wild blueberries
                in the wet slickrock

Night—the spider strings her web
        between the jack pine
                and the crescent moon

AT BOULDER BAY, THE SNAKE SWALLOWING A TOAD

Pine sap has sealed the pen
    to my fingers, insisted
        that the story

be told—how here, in the campsite's cool firepit,
    the slender striped garter snake,
        yellow and black, has clamped

its small mouth around the head
    of a toad, big, brown-spotted, blown
        up tight as a balloon,

his hind feet still scuttling around
    for purchase, a sumo wrestler
        twisting in the hold

of implacable appetite
    unhinging, now, the jaw,
        so that the small head

opens a quarter-inch wider—
    inches short, still,
        of the toad's girth—

slow dance through the ashes
    of hang-on and go-slack
        after the quick strike

from the fissure of rock.
    I step back—whether to offer
        privacy to death

or shield myself
     I can't say, but no chance, I see,
          for the toad,

whether he becomes snake next
     or not—and maybe none for the snake.
          Wind howls and thumps.

I come back an hour later
     to look. The toad's back legs shift
          and pull. The snake's mouth

inches forward another
     quarter inch, jaw unhinges
          another quarter, throat skin

stretches, bulges
     three times its girth, toad head
          and arm stuffed down

that muscled sack, toad
     still blown up tight, snake's tail
          another intelligence, curling

around rock, easing long s-curves of body
     under a ledge. Hours, it takes,
          before the last foot vanishes

down the long rope of digestive track
     and the snake's small eyes blink,
          finished with its impossible task.

QUIET WATER

— *For Will*

We lift the canoe across the beaver dam
of sticks still green with leaves, white bitten tips,
enter the pond of quiet water that stretches flat
before us, six inches higher than the downstream spill,
thick borders of white water lilies—light unfolding
in their petals—reeds, rain clouds dark in the east.

This is our layover day—we are only exploring
the small rivers that link our lake-filled map,
trailing silver vortices in our wake as we cross
the scribing paths of jumping spiders who leap
from one dimpled surface to another on padded feet,
the frantic scribbles of whirligig beetles,
a gossiping in-crowd keeping up with each other,
the rapid, elegant arabesques of waterbugs
in courtship, weaving left, then right, toward
and away from each other with the speed of skaters—
and you and I, plunging steadily along together
into our future,
                    those clouds that reverse direction,
catch us back at camp, spilling rivers of runoff
from the tarp—we rig dams, play in the mud,
channel the rain between us, watch as it dwindles
to a fine tinsel, a silver light in the west, loons
calling, and the double rainbow enters the lake,
crosses the water, ends at our feet.

TOO MUCH FOR ONE THOUGHT TO HOLD,

said Margaret, our lazy day filled to overflow
with the grumble and gleam of fast-changing sky,
the red bunchberries and sphagnum of island trails,
the early morning otter who slipped into ripples,
the cold shock of water on our swimmer's bodies,
rough heat of granite to dry us out. That day we belonged
to the din of rain spattering the lake, to the luminous
orange-pink and violet of sunset, giving way
to the waxing moon; and late at night, we vanished
into fog that muffled sound, erased our camp, leaving
only the red pines standing out black against the mist.

ANECDOTE OF THE FROG

Steadying our canoe we found the frog
    in an overhung cave of fern and moss
curtained by the drip of seeping springs,
    Rana pipiens, spotted, green, tucked back
on a smaller ledge in the fissured rock,
    a small scooped pool a hand-span wide
by which he sat, two inches long,

caught flies, and amplified his luck—
    he filled our sleep with throaty grunts
and snores across the lake, resonant,
    reverberant to the counterpoint
of mosquito whine—no jar;
    belonging there. The wilderness
surrounded him all the same.

ISABELLA LAKE

Loons, rapids, beaver lodge,
kestrels, and light—light
rose and golden climbing
the feathers of clouds, rose
and purple entering the water
reeds, every shade of green
in the blueberry leaves—
and the sting of mosquitoes
as wind dies down with the sun,
as the loon's clamor announces
night coming on....

QUADGA LAKE

At sunset we paddle by the petroglyph
of a moose, full size, on a pyramid
of granite rock rising from the lake,
lichens spotting his hide.
In the little bay,
submerged except for flopping ears
and weed-draped nose,
a moose is eating water lily roots.

At sunrise, the merganser
leads her ducklings three in line
across the morning calm,
only a little ripple left behind
by the eagle who drops to take
the smallest one.

The sleek brown head of a mink,
a fish in its teeth, climbs out;
skirts our feet,
towels, oatmeal bowls
to deliver the bones and scales
to a chatter rising
from under the arborvitae roots.

EDGES

We crossed into wilderness on foot,
　　　　our donkey bodies hung, front and back,
with drysacks, clutching paddles
　　　　and life jackets, the dinner pack,
left behind the gravel parking lot,

entered a rocky portage trail,
　　　　grateful that footing was dry,
remembering times of slogging through mud
　　　　and climbing waterfalls.
Dale and Will shouldered canoes

past miniature forests of club moss,
　　　　boulders rusty with lichen,
the spiky sponges of fruiting moss,
　　　　the edges of marsh—heron stick,
dead pines, black mud.

We searched out tiny wild strawberries
　　　　under saw-toothed leaves, their taste
another edge of wildness,
　　　　intense sweet bursts
that startled springs within the mouth.

To return a week later is another jolt,
　　　　crossing back to the Quik Stop,
leaving behind water flicker and shine,
　　　　wind's voice and cloud race,
star whirl and shoreline.

Our donkey bodies shoulder jobs,
　　　　haul grocery bags from store to car.
At dusk, we go outside to look—
　　　　see the clear-winged sphinx moth
come to the bright pink phlox.

I FIND YOU IN THE WATERY WORLD

— For Will

And it is all motion, water running along the bow of the canoe, motion of ripples off paddle's draw, reflected waves lapping the granite shore—all motion and sound, a motion in the ear, of the rivulets and wash of our progress, the quiet into which we drop, paddles stayed, to hear the otter's bark; the hum of hornets, whine of mosquitoes, rustle of wind in the aspen tops, splatter of rain, the nightly cry-haunted talk of the loons—

Under a sky all change, the clouds' metamorphoses of shape, now horsehead, now billowed cotton balls, now sleek gray shark-strata piling up; the light, picking out one tree, the white of a loon's breast, the lift of a wave, the rose in the granite, the pale ghosts of lichen-hung trees, diamond flashes off the lake, dark with the iron of these waters; sleek bodies of swimmers, the otters' whiskers as they turn to look at us and disappear—

Immersed, we learn to see the dark bottlebrush branches of shoreline jack pine with cones sealed tight; white pine towering in the forest crown, horizontal limbs of soft five-needled whisks; red pine's jagged pairs of three-inch needles littering the ground, covered too by bracken fern and club moss, wintergreen (whose leaves we chew). Reindeer moss and sphagnum, stiff lichen rosettes and spiky sponges, crowd the rock—the sudden red of bunchberry on the path—

Deep in our bodies we trace the motion of wilderness, of morning song, of water washing under us, of sleep on rock, of plunge into the lake's black trough, through the week and back, the next day and the next. In city streets we turn and rock, responsive to wave's pull and thrust; float and bob in the workday world, scanning horizon, listening for wind, for insect hum, still tuned to each other, our progress through a watery world.

ABUNDANCE ❧

SEVEN A.M.

Today the wind has unfastened
Light in the water, opened
The eyes of the dragonfly to see
As many suns as leaves
In slow lap of shadow and gold,

And the branches scarcely contain
Themselves, they shake with light,
They are all dazzle, all motion,
Undone in the very moment of touching,
Dragonfly wings on water,

And then there is no water or wing,
No sun or leaf or watcher,
It has all come apart in the seeing
And we wake up shaken and dazed,
Fallen out of ourselves and the world.

DOUBLE HAPPINESS

Equal measures of daylight and night,
bloom on the pussywillow;
the air, slipping warm over the silver
coolness of the lake, draws up mist
that wets our skin, rolls in low fogbanks
along the shore, and two swans
collecting all the light
drift in the quiet water
where there was only one before.

WALKING THE HALL OF MIRRORS

— Corridor #2, Lucas Samara, for
Will

We step into a world
    repeating ourselves—
here we are behind us,
    looking back, looking back,
all those days waking
    to each other's face,
and here we are below,
    each time standing
head and shoulders
    above ourselves,
offering each other
    a hand-hold,
and here we are above, hovering
    in a floating cloud
of heavenly selves
    smiling down on us,
and here we are shoulder
    to shoulder on either side,
companions as we move forward
    to welcome
ourselves coming toward us
    in uncountable numbers
advancing with hands outstretched,
    so many of you smiling
at me, so many of me
    smiling at you.

DANCERS

— For RWC

Light and shadow
Blend
In the polished bronze

Two figures mirror
To each other
Joining hands, swaying
In the surface light

All one,
Nothing to know the body by
But its grace,
The way it bends the light

WILD PLUM

Wet meadow, dry hill, the black burnt stubs
of broom grass, Queen Anne's lace and thistle
stalks; we space the bushel bags of chaff
and seed—grass or forbs—every fifty yards,
fill our pails, sow this new burn on the Ice
Age Trail. Wind winnows straw and dust
from the flung harvest threshed at Hook Lake
prairie. Dun and yellow seeds speckle ash
as we criss-cross the acres: these will be
scarified in winter ice, loosen in spring
to root as prairie smoke, yellow puccoon,
rough blazing star, spiderwort, turkeyfoot
and little bluestem—a hundred more. We grow
prickly with straw-filled mouths and hair,
teary-eyed with dust, work steadily on
to the song of flickers, magnolia warblers
passing through, the early spring perfume
of the wild plum hedgerow in massed white bloom.

BY THE WISCONSIN RIVER

Walk the old logging trails
through the spring woods,
six miles out to the spine of the ridgeline,
walk the tractor paths overlooking the river
six miles back to the bluff and road.

Walk the deer trails through the underbrush,
walk through the aspens just showing their green
and the carpets of leaf mold,
walk through the red of the poison ivy leaflets,
the whiplash of raspberry canes.

Walk through the prairie's first showing
of pussytoes, puccoon, and bird's foot violets,
walk through the tick-ridden grasses,
walk through the wild phlox
and unfurling ferns of maidenhair.

Walk through the cloudshapes
moving on turned fields,
walk through the sunsoaked uplands,
the lilacs of old foundations,
the white light of wild plum at wood-edge.

Walk the river margin, sandhills calling,
walk through the morning, walk through afternoon—
return with empty hands to the city.
Dream into the long green well of walking
that opens now whenever your eyes close.

THE HILL IN MARQUETTE COUNTY

The rain barrel has collapsed into a sheaf
of curved boards held loosely in rusted loops.
How many years since I sat on this rock,
watching young sons at play in the sandblow,
watching the redheaded woodpeckers
feeding their young in the dead oak tree
by the fence line? Or later, the fledglings
learning to fly while my own hung skyward
in loops of three-hundred sixty degrees before
they plunged again downwards to meet
the plywood ramp they'd built in the meadow
of needle grass. It stands silvery now
after the thunderstorm, splintered wood
with its curves still smooth, the four-by-fours
stepping off their sturdy measures of arc,
well-made as the homes drilled year after year.
The sons plunge into their twenty-something
years, tattoo artist, brewmaster who calls this
the summer of love, though the limbs of the oak
have fallen now, the cedar shakes blown
from the shelter's roof.
                              I want to cry *sorry, sorry,*
for the world I let fall away but the field
will have none of the story—the sandblow's grown up
into pepper grass and juniper, field sparrows sing
from the blighted oak trunk, jeweled gold-and-green
flies buzz in June heat—no place less abandoned
than this. Nor did I forget the sky, its rainbows
and storms, its fledgling birds, its blond boys
turning in widening arc, bound now in memory's hoop.

WHAT'S LEFT OUT

In my notes, only a trace of that day with Will: *the deer at the riverbank, otter, turtles of the Namekagon, rain on the Totagatik; Coney Island Chili Hotdogs with Root Beer Floats.*

The deer who stepped into current, swam to the other side, vanished into woods—I did not write down the hesitation before he entered the river, the way the water opened and closed again behind him, the way his hooves scraped the muddy bank and the water dripped off his flanks.

And the otter who popped up behind our canoe, watching our progress down the Namekagon—the wet slick of his head, his brown eyes, the otter's name for the river something else—*River That Brings Trout*, perhaps.

Nor did I praise sufficiently the turtles, sunning themselves on logs and rocks, lineups and rafts of turtles who stretched their necks out like old men on a bench by the courthouse, eyes half-closed taking everything in, then tumbling off as our shadows approached.

And I did not record, on the Totagatik, the way the rain pebbled the water in little cratered bursts splashing up, sending the whirligig beetles, with their two pairs of eyes that see above and below, whirling and skittering over the skin of the river.

Nor the way the ice cream foamed.

THE TERRITORY OF HORSES

Suppose I looked at you
And you looked away? Or stayed?

Our eyes the way we have of moving,
The way a horse, in moving,

Will school another;
So says the girl who spent three summers

In the canyon with the mustangs
And learned to be a horse—

How to move around the territory
Finding water, grass, and shelter,

The herd watching to see
What she knew in these matters.

How to greet another quickly touching
A nose and veering off.

Running at the ones
Skittish enough to move

At the sound of the rattle and whipcrack
She trailed behind her.

How to stand by the other's heart
The way a colt will shadow its mother.

How to ask the other
To walk beside her in the way she moved.

How she led the whole herd out
Three summers later, dipping and raising her head.

What horses say to one another, standing deep
In grass, with their great arched necks.

HOLDING ON

Trees have learned the trick of it,
Letting go all those leaves
For the green sap, the scaly bud,
A few berries or winged seeds held
Through the dark months, saving
What counts in a new time.

When branches go, sap feeds a few
New shoots every year. Bark sluffs
To show the work of worms. Woodpeckers
Take up residence in the bare trunk.
Fallen, the tree becomes rainbreak,
Badger den. Listen, in a green time

I was all rustle and shade for you;
In a bare time, you will find shelter here;
Past time, bloodroot will thicken here.

FALL AT VILAS PARK

Lily pads stand up, wave goodbye to the bridge.
Canada geese—a flotilla of periscoped necks
Prepared to submerge—drift into the cool breeze
That shivers the water, disturbs the leaves.

On the lawn, the shrieks of children chasing balls,
Screech of the swing set, slow casts of the lazy
Fishermen watching the gulls, the sun's rays,
Blue sky over us all. Maple-hearted, oak-thighed,

I stride through leaves. True colors bleed through
now that green is going—surely
My bones will be birch when I let go my body,
Another white body in the dark woods.

ENOUGH

There is always enough.
My old cat of long years, who
stayed all the months of his dying,

though, made sick by food,
he refused to eat, till, long-stroked,
he turned again to accept

another piece of dry catfood
or spoonful of meat, a little water,
another day through which

he purred, small engine
losing heat—I made him nests
of pillow and blanket, a curve of body

where he curled against my legs,
and when the time came, he slipped out
a loose door into the cold world

whose abundance included
the death of his choosing.

DAILINESS

It is the birds
　　who call me back
　　　　to the world

Animation of sparrows
　　among arbor vitae branches
　　　　in my morning dash with the dog

Brief glimpse of geese
　　crying their ragged way across sky
　　　　as I wait in traffic

Waxwings busy
　　stripping the small red crabapples
　　　　beside my office building's door

Crows calling after me
　　as I leave, *pay attention, pay*
　　　　attention, pay attention

To what is slipping away

WISH FOR THE NEW YEAR

Ghosts on the marsh
Making their slow way, ice skating
That strangely changed
Surface, they cross the middle
In stiffnecked wobble, summer swans
Who've stayed past sense,
Past solstice, a white pair
Who made this marsh surround them here,
Whose slow drift, always together,
Their lovely necks wrapped around each other,
Or gravely bowed, tamed the water.

Now their great wings rise,
Circle the frozen marsh,
Vanish again toward the closing lake.
Oh, may the harsh winds coming carry them
To open water; may they find shelter
Among the last geese calling and crying
A way to southern weather;
May they survive against the odds together.

THESE ARE THE WORDS FOR MORNING

These are the words for morning: holy
　　the sun entering the world through the limbs
　　　　of the maples, the oaks,
its long rays glancing off new leaves,
　　the lake. Even the stones, from which we come,
　　　　are holy, the mud and ruck and rack
of weeds at the edge of the marsh,
　　seedbed to water and bank. Holy the clouds
　　　　in their gold and white feathers,
holy the birds who have sung up the lightening sky,
　　the cardinal foremost on the tip of the spruce,
　　　　the white-throated sparrow's sweet cascade
through our morning dreams; holy the alarm call
　　of the chipmunk, sighting the last predator
　　　　of night, our hunting cat heading home;
holy the cat. Holy the mother raccoon
　　and her children, fat with sunflower seed,
　　　　vanishing into the sewer; the woodchuck
stirring under the porch, thinking of dandelion heads;
　　holy the spider catching dew in her web,
　　　　the mud-dauber wasp beginning her work;
the apple trees loosening their buds.
　　Holy the newsboy making his rounds,
　　　　the bus driver starting his route,
holy the bus, the rabbits cropping the greening grass;
　　holy this house; the entering fingers of dawn;
　　　　holy the two of us holding each other,
the water we rise to, bread and fruit.
　　Holy each of earth's creatures, opening to day.
　　　　Holy each creature sinking to sleep.

THERE IS SOMETHING TO BE SAID

For winter, how its black and white
Light strips summer away
To show what was hidden
Under the green leaf—old scaffold
Of branch and trunk, brushy
Upstart stem—how, after the fact,
We discover the places where wild birds
Lived, walk the woods marveling
At how open it all is,
And how simple, believing, surely,
In the green of a new year
We can find our way back again.

ABUNDANCE

Yes, write of it, here right now,
in the middle of winter, snow
pock-marked with tracks
of squirrels and the backyard rabbit,
mice that spiral the long grass
into nests, the pair of cardinals
who own the house and all the trees
surrounding it, the raccoon family
from the water drain at the end
of the block (their eyes gleam
through the sewer grate on cold
night walks) who stop on their own
nightly rounds to pour the feeder seed
down their throats, the housefinches
from the front porchlight, heads
soaked in berry-red, foraging leftovers,
the chickadees dry and two-note calling
in the arborvitae, finishing off from a claw
the single sunflower seed that each
takes to a branch: we are wealthy,
wealthy in the black oil of seed, the gold
of cracked corn, the brushy thickets
of security from cats, the abundant lives
of our neighbors.

HAPPINESS,

the elusive, the longed-for, the ever-receding,
arriving when all your tasks in the world are done,
when the basement is clean enough to dance in,
when the photographs have all been put into albums,
when the yard has all been turned into garden,
when the thousands of numbers in the research project
have been cast into words, and the thousands of words
in poems have been folded into books, when the books
are read and alphabetized on their shelves, when

the man arrives who will dance with you in the clean
basement, his dark good looks and sophisticated tango
giving away his name as he takes you, so old that
the faces, the flowers, the numbers, the words,
the books have all blurred, into his arms—even then,
happiness will still be there, faithful by your side,
waiting, as it has always waited, hovering, hoping
to be seen—as it waits by each of us, the whole
of our extraordinary, our only, our human, lives.

ACKNOWLEDGEMENTS

꒜

With gratitude to the Leighton Studios, Banff Centre for the Arts, Canada, for winter time and space to work on poems; and to the 2001 Symposium on Writing and the Natural World, Centre for Rural Studies and Enrichment, St. Peter's College, Saskatchewan, Canada, facilitated by Tim Lilburn and Don McKay, for their discussion of the poetics of nature writing. With thanks to my manuscript groups for acute listening and comment. And with special thanks to the following publications in which these poems first appeared:

Appalachia: Cattails; Isabella Lake; Bloodroot.
Ascent: Field Trip.
ByLine Magazine: What's Left Out.
The Christian Science Monitor: The Marsh as Weathercock; Prairie Restoration; If Crickets Didn't Sing; Dancers; Turkeyfoot.
Earth's Daughters: By Campfire Light.
Export: Writing the Midwest, (BigBridge.org.): The Hill in Marquette County.
Free Verse: Anecdote of the Frog.
The Hudson Review: Wild Sarsaparilla.
Kalliope: For Dinner We Had Potatoes.
The Middlewesterner Blog: By the Wisconsin River; Quadga Lake.
Nimrod: Crossing the Bog.
Northeast: Double Happiness; At Boulder Bay, the Snake Swallowing the Toad.
Poetry East: Walking the Hall of Mirrors.
Poet Lore: There is Something to Be Said.
Prairie Schooner: Madison, 3/8.
Prairie Winds: The Territory of Horses.
SnowApple: I Find You in the Watery World; Prairie.
The Southern Poetry Review: Wild Indigo.
The Southern Review: Wish for the New Year.
White Pelican Review: These Are the Words for Morning.
Wisconsin Academy Review: The Evolution of Sleep; What the Eye Supplies.
Wisconsin Poets' Calendar: Braiding; Dailiness; Seven A.M.; Burning the Prairie.
WordWrights!: Sadness.
Yankee: Fall at Vilas Park; Holding On; Passage.

About the
Cider Press Review
Book Award

First Prize: $1,000 and Publication of Book
2009 Judge: David St. John

- Manuscripts can be submitted by mail or online using the entry form at **ciderpressreview.com/bookaward**
- Submit 48-80 pages of original poetry in English not previously published in full-length book form (individual poems may have been previously published in journals, anthologies and chapbooks)
- Manuscripts must be postmarked or submitted online between September 1 and November 30 of the contest year
- For mail submissions, enclose 2 title pages: Name, mailing address, phone number and email should appear on the first title page only
- For online submissions include title page with title of manuscript only
- Manuscript should be typed, single-spaced, paginated and bound with a spring clip
- Include a table of contents page(s) and an acknowledgements page listing previous publication credits
- Enclose an SASE with mailed manuscript for announcement of winner only
- Electronic submissions will be notified via email only
- Include a check or money order for $25 payable to Cider Press Review, or remit entry fee via PayPal
- **Manuscripts cannot be returned**
- All entries will receive a copy of the winning book

Mail to:

Cider Press Review Book Award
777 Braddock Lane
Halifax, PA 17032

For more information, visit **ciderpressreview.com**